Conten

GW01017764

2- 3 Introduction

4- 5 What you'll need

6- 9 Getting started

10- 15 Technique #1 - Dots

16- 21 Technique #2 - Accordion fold

22- 27 Technique #3 - Spiral

28- 33 Technique #4 - Bullseye

34- 39 Technique #5 - Triangle fold

40- 45 Technique #6 - Crumple

46- 47 Why not try?

GET
STARTED
TODAY

Introduction

Tie-dye is the method of folding, twisting or crumpling fabric and securing with elastic bands before applying bright, colourful dyes. The dye cannot penetrate the areas under the elastic bands, causing bold patterns.

The tie-dye style is often associated with the 1970's, but actually it existed long before this era. Shibori is a Japanese term referring to a variety of resist-dye techniques which have been used around the world for over 6000 years.

Following the different tie-dye methods in this book, you can control the effects of the dye to an extent. However, the fun and excitement of tie-dye all comes from the surprise when you untie your unique creation! It's almost impossible to get tie-dye wrong.

We've included two cotton napkins as a base material to get you started. There is a napkin project on page 10, but you can use any other method in the book to try out your favourite style.

Get experimenting and see what you can create!

What you'll need

Dye

Colour is the most important part of tie-dye! You can experiment with lots of different effects; stick to one colour for a more sophisticated, marbled look, or use a variety to embrace the rainbow excitement of tie-dye!

We've included 3 powdered dyes in this kit, pre-measured in applicator bottles to help you get started quickly and easily.

If you want to buy more dye to try out new techniques, just remember to consider what kind of fabric you are using, and make sure to get a suitable dye. Whichever you choose, remember to read the manufacturer's directions carefully before use.

TIP The 'direct application' method works best for tie-dye, so wash out the applicator bottles when empty, ready to re-use!

Material

You can use lots of different blanks as a base for your tie-dye projects, but remember that dye will take better to certain fabrics. Cotton, linen and viscose fabrics will always work best. You can also tie-dye on wool, silk and polyester/cotton blends, but bear in mind the end result will be less vibrant.

We recommend you avoid using 100% polyester, acrylic and nylon fabrics, or those with any kind of special coating or finish. The dye will not take properly to these synthetic materials.

T-shirts, tote bags, pillow cases and tea-towels are all great options for tie-dying; collect together lots of blanks so you can try out all the different effects!

Elastic bands

These simple bands are crucial for creating those characteristic patterns. We've included some for you, but you can also experiment with thicker or thinner bands to achieve a slightly different look. You can re-use these as many times as you like so keep hold of them!

Gloves

Always wear protective gloves when tie-dying to avoid staining your skin.

Getting Started

WARNING!

Instructions for other manufacturer's dyes may differ. If using different dyes, read and follow the instructions on the packaging carefully.

HOW-TO

The general process is the same for each of the methods used in this book. Follow the steps below for each project, adapting step 2 according to which technique you wish to use.

STEP 1

Dye takes better to clean, wet fabric, so wash your blank as normal before you begin and leave it damp.

STEP 2

Lay the fabric flat on your covered work surface.
Prepare your fabric according to the technique you'd like to follow, using the projects within the book for inspiration.

STEP 3

Unscrew the lid of the applicator bottle and remove the sachet of powdered dye. Empty the powder into the bottle and fill with warm water from the tap. The water will froth when added to the powdered dye, so add very slowly and carefully.

STEP 4

Replace the cap tightly and securely. Shake the bottle well until the powdered dye has completely dissolved.

STEP 5

Apply dye directly to the fabric using the applicator nozzle. Be careful not to oversaturate the material, as this could lead to the dye seeping into folds and under the elastic bands.

STEP 6

Add extra colours if desired. Remember if you add a second colour touching the first, you'll end up with a third where the two mix! Leave a slight gap in between if you don't want the colours to mix.

STEP 7
Once you are happy with the dye application, wrap the fabric in cling film. This will prevent it from drying out.

STEP 8
Leave the fabric in the cling film for 6-8 hours.

STEP 9
Rinse the fabric in cold water. Do this in the sink, under the tap, and keep going until the water starts to run clear.

STEP 10
Remove the elastic bands.

STEP 11
Hand-wash the fabric in warm water with a small amount of detergent. It's normal for more colour to come out of the fabric at this stage.

STEP 12

Hang out the fabric and leave to dry naturally, away from direct sunlight or sources of heat.

IMPORTANT

Always wash your tie-dyed fabrics separately for the first few washes to ensure any excess dye is removed without accidentally colouring the other items you are washing. Do not allow dyed fabric to rest wet on any other items as colour could be transferred.

TOP TIPS

Keep these in mind before you begin.

- Do not mix the powdered dye with water until you are ready to use it. Dye left unapplied after 24 hours will begin to lose concentration and will result in a weaker colour result.

- Make sure your work surface is prepared before you start. Tie-dying can be very messy! Cover your surface with a plastic sheet or newspaper, and wear old clothes or an apron. Have everything you need to hand.

- When creating geometric designs, remember every fold you make will create a white line in your fabric. It's worth spending some time on these folds before adding the dye. Think about how you want your finished piece to look. Use narrow folds for smaller patterns and wider folds for larger patterns.

- Of course, you can embrace the more organic look. Crumpling, scrunching and twisting will create more free-flowing designs.

- Tie those elastic bands really tightly. They stop the dye getting underneath so the more secure they are, the cleaner your finished patterns will be.

- Always stick with primary colours when combining; some secondary colours will blend together into muddy brown shades! Try to maintain a distance between secondary colours if you want to use them on the same fabric.

- Remember to apply dye to the back of the fabric as well as the front if you want a double-sided design.

Technique #1

DOTS

Liven up some plain white napkins for your next dinner party with a fun, dotty design! This simple method is done by tying off small sections of fabric.

Before

After

MAKE THESE NAPKINS WITH THE CONTENTS OF YOUR KIT!

STEP 1

Prepare your fabric and lay it flat on your work surface.

STEP 2

Pull up small sections of fabric and secure tightly with elastic bands.

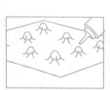

STEP 3

Apply the dye to the fabric, squeezing the bottle gently and slowly to ensure you don't add too much dye and oversaturate the material. Be particularly careful near the elastic bands, otherwise the dye could seep in underneath.

STEP 4

Wrap in cling film and leave for 6-8 hours before rinsing and washing (refer to the main instructions on page 6-9).

TIPS

- Use just 1 colour to enjoy the simple white circles left by the elastic bands.

- To create a polka dot effect, dye the pinched sections one colour, and the rest of the fabric a second colour.

- Add 2 or more complementary shades and apply sporadically all over the fabric for an organic look.

YOU CAN ALSO TRY

- Tie the fabric off in neat lines for a uniform dotty effect.

- Go more scattered for a free-flowing look.

- Make some pinched sections longer than others and add more than one elastic band to these. This will create different sized circles across your fabric.

Technique #2

Accordion Fold

Vest tops are a great choice for tie-dye; they're cheap to pick up and you can create your own unique fashion. It's a really fun activity to try on a variety of garments so see what you can find!

This folding method creates a wonderful geometric design.

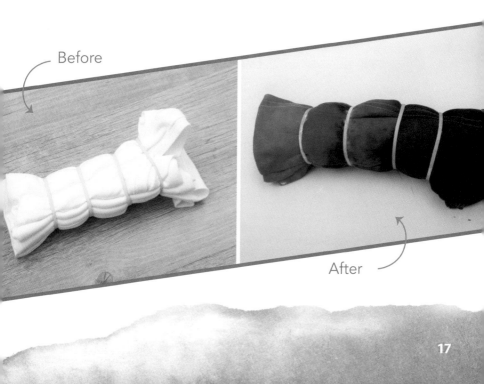

Before

After

STEP 1
Prepare your fabric and lay it flat on your
work surface.

STEP 2
Fold the fabric in half lengthways to create a long,
thin piece.

STEP 3
Starting from the bottom, begin to accordion fold the fabric. Thi
means to alternate the way you fold each time in order to create
pleats that resemble an accordion.
Take your time over these folds, making sure each panel is the
same size and that your creases are neat and crisp.

STEP 4
Continue folding all the way up until you are left with a rectangle
of fabric.

STEP 5
Secure the folded fabric with a number of elastic bands up the
length.

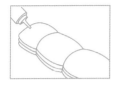

STEP 6
Apply the dye to the fabric, being careful to add dye to the folds on each side.

STEP 7
Wrap in cling film and leave for 6-8 hours before rinsing and washing (refer to the main instructions on page 6-9).

TIPS

- Use indigo blue dye for a traditional Shibori look.

- Alternate 2 colours on each section separated by the elastic bands.

- For a multi-coloured surprise when you unfold, apply a different colour to each section. This looks great in rainbow colours!

YOU CAN ALSO TRY

- Each fold creates a line in the pattern, so go small for a more intricate design or use larger folds for a bolder pattern.

- Add more elastic bands to add extra detail.

Technique #3

SPIRAL

This is probably the method that springs to most people's minds when they think of tie-dye. The spiral is bold, eye-catching and usually seen boasting a myriad of colours. It works really well on a white t-shirt, but you can try it on any other fabric you have too!

Before

After

STEP 1

Prepare your fabric and lay it flat on your work surface.

STEP 2

Think about where you want the centre of the design to be; it's normally the middle of the fabric, but it could be wherever you want! Pinch the fabric at your chosen centre and twist the remaining fabric around this point. Keep going until all the fabric has been wound into a rough swirl.

STEP 3

Bind together with elastic bands to create triangular wedge shapes. The traditional design consists of 6 wedges created with 3 elastic bands.

STEP 4

Apply dye to each wedge section in turn. Start with the lightest colours, and be careful not to muddy them together if you want distinct, bright colours.

STEP 5

Wrap in cling film and leave for 6-8 hours before rinsing and washing (refer to the main instructions on page 6-9).

TIPS

- This design suits lots of bright colours. Add a different dye to each wedge in order of the rainbow e.g. blue, green, yellow, orange, red, pink.

- For a more subtle design, you can try alternating 2 colours between the wedges.

- Pick a few colours that go well together and blend the dyes between each wedge to create an ombre effect.

YOU CAN ALSO TRY

- Use 3 bands to create the traditional 6 wedges or you can experiment with more or less depending on how many colours you wish to use.

Technique #4

Bullseye

Another well recognised tie-dye technique is the bullseye which creates rings of colour for a spectacular finish. We've used a plain, large piece of hemmed cotton fabric. Perfect for brightening tables and sideboards in rented accommodation, university halls or just as a feature to hang with pride in your lounge!

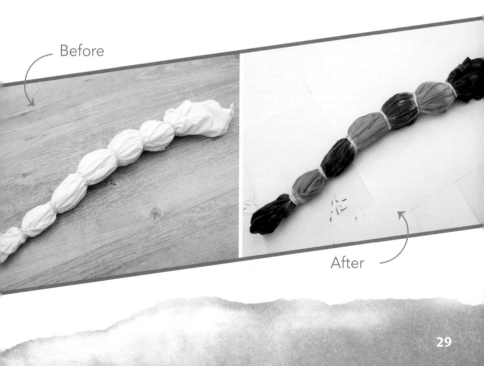

Before

After

STEP 1

Prepare your fabric and lay it flat on your work surface.

STEP 2

Decide on where the centre of your design will be and pull a section upwards into a tube shape from this point.

STEP 3

Secure rubber bands along the length of the tube.

STEP 4

Apply dye to each section of fabric.

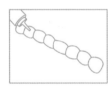

STEP 5

Wrap in cling film and leave for 6-8 hours before rinsing and washing (refer to the main instructions on page 6-9).

TIPS

- Use a variety of colours on each section for a bold design.

- Pick a colour and work through a range of shades from light to dark for an ombre effect.

- Alternate 2 different shades; pick your favourite colours!

YOU CAN ALSO TRY

- Add more elastic bands for lots of thin circles, or less for a chunkier look.

- Play with the distances between the elastic bands; include wider sections and some thinner ones to see what happens!

- Only add elastic bands at the tip of the tube and leave the rest a solid colour. This will create a more subtle pattern in the middle of your fabric.

Technique #5

Triangle fold

Similar to the accordion fold, this method produces a beautiful geometric pattern reminiscent of ancient Shibori styles. Pillow cases are a great item to try the triangle fold with as they allow for more folds than a smaller piece of fabric would. Add some real pizzazz to your bedroom, or try cotton cushion covers instead to brighten up any space.

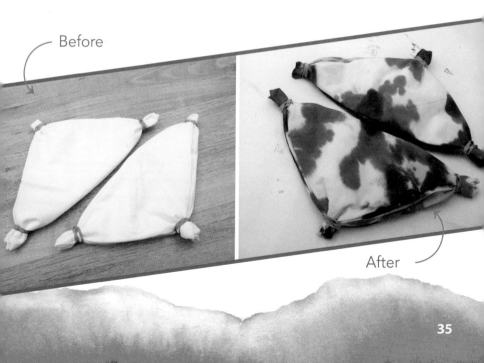

Before

After

STEP 1

Prepare your fabric and lay it flat on your work surface.

STEP 2

Fold the fabric in half lengthways to create a long strip.

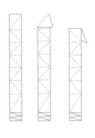

STEP 3

Fold the strip accordion style, but in triangles rather than square panels. To do this, start at one end and pull the top outer corner down to the bottom of the strip, keeping the fabric edges square as you go to create a triangle.

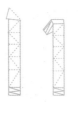

STEP 4

Continue folding up the length of the strip, alternating the direction you fold each time to create equal triangular panels. You should be left with a triangular shape at the end.

STEP 5

Tie off each of the three corners with elastic bands to secure the fabric together.

STEP 6

Apply the dye to the triangle, paying particular attention to the folded edges.

STEP 7

Wrap in cling film and leave for 6-8 hours before rinsing and washing (refer to the main instructions on page 6-9).

TIPS

- Add 1 colour to the main fabric and another on the secure corners.

- Marble complementary colours across the fabric at random.

YOU CAN ALSO TRY

- Fold your fabric in half lengthways again at step 2 to create a thinner strip. This will result in smaller triangles for a more intricate design.

- Instead of tying the corners, run elastic bands over the fabric. Do this evenly or at random to create different effects on your finished piece.

- Add a triangular piece of cardboard to the centre of the folded fabric and secure with elastic bands for an extra level of resistance.

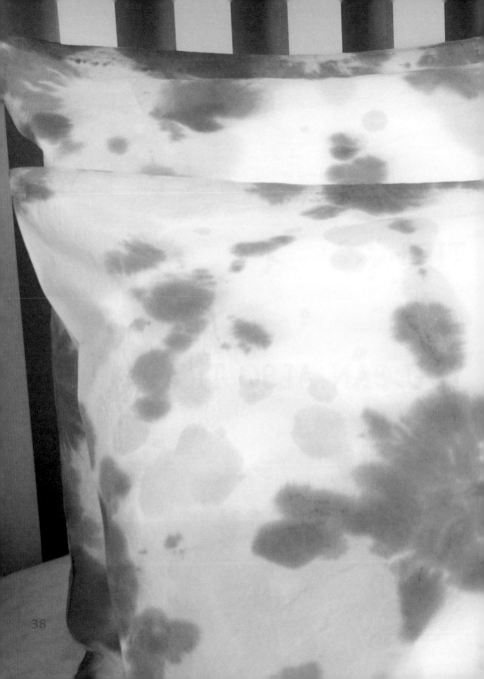

Technique #6

Crumble

Once prepped for dying, this method resembles the spiral. However, it creates a very different end result! This is perhaps the most organic looking of all the methods in this book, as it's arguably the least contrived. We've tried out the crumple technique on a recycled cotton tote bag, to create a usable item that still celebrates that unique, tie-dyed effect!

Before

After

STEP 1

Prepare your fabric and lay it flat on your work surface.

STEP 2

Scrunch the fabric using your fingers. You can be very rough with this – just pinch, grab and crumple the fabric up into a ball!

STEP 3

Secure in a similar way to the spiral method, wrapping as many elastic bands around the crumpled ball as you desire. Try not to add these too symmetrically (as you would with a spiral) as this will reduce the natural look we're aiming for.

STEP 4

Apply the dye to the fabric.

STEP 5

Wrap in cling film and leave for 6-8 hours before rinsing and washing (refer to the main instructions on page 6-9).

TIPS

- Keep colours simple to embrace the organic feel of this method.

- Add more than 1 colour and rub the fabric with your fingers (while wearing gloves, of course!) to blend the colours more evenly.

- Use 2 shades of the same colour for a standout yet simple look.

YOU CAN ALSO TRY

- Try combining the crumple technique with other methods; tie off sections for the dots method then crumple up and secure the rest of the fabric on the opposite side.

Why not try...

If you've got to grips with the process of tie-dying, you may want to experiment with other ways of creating patterns rather than just using elastic bands. There are lots of ideas out there using basic materials you may have lying around the house!

STRING

Roll, scrunch or fold the fabric, then wrap a long length of string tightly around it. Wrap sparingly or generously; evenly or sporadically; see what effects you can create!

MARBLES

To create neat, white circular designs on dyed fabric, place a marble underneath the fabric and cinch the material over it with a rubber band. Repeat with additional marbles in your desired pattern. Using different sized marbles will create larger or smaller circles.

STITCHES

Draw straight lines onto the fabric with a water-soluble marker. Sew long running stitches along these lines using a needle and thread. Pull the thread ends to bunch the fabric up before adding the dye. The dye will resist the areas slightly where the thread and bunching is.

PEGS

Fold the fabric into small pleats and hold in place with pegs. You can also combine pegs with elastic bands, by tying off tufts of fabric then securing pleats of fabric with pegs in a circular design around the tuft.

CARDBOARD OR WOODEN BLOCKS

Small, thin wooden blocks are perfect for creating repeat geometric designs. Accordion-fold the fabric lengthwise, then fold again to make a square. Place a wooden block (or thick cardboard) on one side of the fabric and secure with rubber bands. If you use a block smaller than your fabric square, you'll get lots of chunky coloured sections in the finished piece. A block the same size as your fabric square will create thin lines of colour and lots of white space.

Author

A2V

Published By

A2V

DESIGNED IN
DORSET

Produced responsibly in China.
© A2V, Longham Business Park,
168 Ringwood Rd, Ferndown, BH22 9BU.
© A2V, 77 Lower Camden Street, St Kevin's,
Dublin 2, Ireland, D02 XE 80.
Company Number: 8102350 www.a2v.com
Third Edition, First Print